# WONDERS OF CREATION

## THE SOUL OF THE OCEAN

### APRIL WILSON

# TABLE OF CONTENTS



# CHAPTER 1

## THE OCEAN

The ocean, vast and awe-inspiring, is a breathtaking canvas that covers more than 70% of our planet's surface. It stretches across endless horizons, hiding depths yet to be fully explored, and harboring a world of wonders beyond imagination. With its ever-changing shades of blue, from tranquil cerulean to tempestuous indigo, the ocean has captured the hearts and minds of humanity throughout history.

At first glance, the ocean appears as a serene expanse, a place of tranquility where waves gently caress sandy shores and sunlight dances upon its surface. But beneath this seemingly peaceful facade lies a realm of unparalleled beauty and mystery. The ocean teems with a symphony of life, a vibrant tapestry of creatures and ecosystems that have adapted and evolved over millions of years.

Dive beneath the surface, and a mesmerizing world unveils itself. Coral reefs, resplendent with an explosion of colors, house an intricate network of marine life. Swarms of fish, resolute in their unity, glide effortlessly through sunlit waters. Graceful sea turtles navigate with ancient wisdom, while majestic whales embark on epic migrations that span vast distances. Delicate seahorses, adorned with intricate patterns, enchant with their delicate nature.

Venturing deeper, into the abyssal depths, the ocean reveals a realm of darkness and enigma. Bioluminescent creatures light up the inky blackness, casting an ethereal glow upon the waters. Towering kelp forests sway in a slow-motion ballet, providing shelter for an array of fascinating organisms. Mysterious creatures, such as the colossal giant squid, lurk in the shadows, their existence shrouded in secrecy.

But the ocean is not just a realm of breathtaking beauty—it is also a vital lifeline for our planet. It acts as a colossal regulator of Earth's climate, absorbing vast amounts of carbon dioxide and generating a significant portion of the oxygen we breathe. The ocean's currents and temperatures influence weather patterns and help to stabilize our climate. It sustains livelihoods and provides sustenance to millions of people around the world through fishing and tourism.

However, the ocean faces immense challenges. Human activities, such as pollution, overfishing, and climate change, threaten its delicate balance. Plastic waste litters its shores and endangers marine 9life while rising temperatures and acidification threaten coral reefs and marine ecosystems. It is our collective responsibility to protect and preserve this fragile treasure, to ensure that future generations can continue to marvel at its wonders.

The ocean's allure transcends its vastness and its mysteries. It has the power to captivate our senses, awaken our curiosity, and remind us of the profound interconnectedness of all life on Earth. It beckons us to explore its depths, embrace its beauty, and recognize our role as stewards of its well-being.

It consists of several major divisions, including the Pacific, Atlantic, Indian, Southern, and Arctic Oceans. The average depth of the ocean is approximately 12,080 feet (3,682 meters), but it can vary significantly depending on the location. The deepest part of the ocean is the Mariana Trench in the western Pacific, which reaches a staggering depth of about 36,070 feet (10,972 meters).

The ocean is made up of saltwater and has a number of unique physical characteristics. It is divided into three main layers: the surface layer, the thermocline, and the deep ocean. The surface layer is the top layer of the ocean, which extends from the surface down to about 200 meters (656 feet). This layer is influenced by the atmosphere and is the warmest and most well-lit part of the ocean.

Below the surface layer is the thermocline, a region where the temperature of the water decreases rapidly with depth. The thermocline extends from about 200 to 1000 meters (656 to 3281 feet). The deep ocean is the lowest layer of the ocean and extends from 1000 meters (3281 feet) down to the ocean floor. The deep ocean is the coldest and most pressure-filled part of the ocean.

There are many different types of ocean habitats, each with its own unique set of inhabitants. Coral reefs, for example, are found in tropical and subtropical waters and are home to a diverse range of colorful and exotic sea creatures, including fish, coral, and invertebrates.

The deep sea is the lowest part of the ocean and is home to strange and unusual creatures that have adapted to life in the extreme conditions found there. Pelagic animals live in the open water of the ocean, while coastal and estuarine animals can be found in the shallow waters along the coast.

The ocean is home to a wide variety of sea creatures, including fish, mollusks, crustaceans, marine mammals, and many others. These creatures play important roles in the ocean ecosystem, from serving as primary producers at the bottom of the food chain to being top predators.

The ocean is home to a diverse array of life forms, making it one of the most biologically rich ecosystems on the planet. From tiny microorganisms to gigantic whales, the ocean hosts a wide range of organisms. Some fascinating inhabitants include:

Phytoplankton: These microscopic plants float near the surface and serve as the foundation of the ocean's food chain. They produce a significant amount of the Earth's oxygen and play a crucial role in regulating the climate.

Coral Reefs: These unique ecosystems are formed by colonies of tiny animals called coral polyps. They provide habitat for numerous species of fish, crustaceans, and other marine organisms. Coral reefs are often referred to as the "rainforests of the sea" due to their incredible biodiversity.

Giant Squid: These deep-sea dwellers are known for their enormous size and mysterious nature. They can grow up to 43 feet (13 meters) in length and have the largest eyes of any known animal. Despite their size, they are elusive and have rarely been observed in their natural habitat.

Blue Whale: As the largest animal to have ever existed on Earth, blue whales are truly awe-inspiring. They can reach lengths of up to 98 feet (30 meters) and weigh around 200 tons. These gentle giants primarily feed on small shrimp-like creatures called krill.

The volume of the ocean refers to the total amount of water it contains. The estimated volume of the global ocean is approximately 1.332 billion cubic kilometers. This immense volume of water influences the Earth's climate by absorbing and redistributing heat, and it acts as a massive reservoir for storing carbon dioxide.

Salinity: The ocean is not just comprised of water; it also contains various dissolved salts and minerals. On average, the salinity of the ocean is around 3.5%, meaning that about 3.5% of the ocean's mass is made up of dissolved salts. This salinity level can vary in different regions due to factors such as evaporation, precipitation, and freshwater input from rivers.

Deep Water Formation: The ocean's volume is not uniformly distributed. Deep water formation occurs in certain regions, particularly near the poles, where surface waters become dense and sink to the depths. This process contributes to the global oceanic circulation, known as the thermohaline circulation, which helps regulate Earth's climate.

Seawater Pressure: As you descend deeper into the ocean, the pressure increases significantly. At approximately 10 meters of depth, the pressure is about twice that of the Earth's atmospheric pressure. At the deepest parts of the ocean, such as the Mariana Trench, the pressure can be over 1,000 times greater than at the surface. Such extreme pressures pose unique challenges for exploring the deep-sea environment.

These fun facts about the ocean, its depth, inhabitants, and volume provide just a glimpse into the wonders of this vast and diverse ecosystem. Exploring and understanding the ocean is an ongoing endeavor that continues to reveal new discoveries and insights

Let us cherish the ocean, for within its depths lies a profound source of inspiration, wonder, and life. May it forever remain a symbol of our planet's resilience, reminding us of the boundless possibilities that lie within our reach if we tread lightly and protect this irreplaceable treasure.

# CHAPTER 2

## OCEAN INHABITANTS

There are many different types of habitats in the ocean, each with its own unique set of inhabitants. Here are a few examples:

Coral reefs: These are underwater structures made up of coral and other organisms such as algae and mollusks. Coral reefs are home to a wide variety of animals, including fish, sea turtles, octopuses, and many others.

Estuaries: These are areas where freshwater from rivers and streams mixes with saltwater from the ocean. Estuaries are home to a variety of animals, including crabs, shrimp, and many species of fish.

Open ocean: The open ocean is the vast expanse of the ocean that is not near the coast. It is home to many animals, including whales, dolphins, sharks, and various species of fish.

Deep sea: The deep sea is the part of the ocean that is below the photic zone, where there is no sunlight. It is a very cold and dark environment and is home to a variety of animals such as deep-sea fish, squid, and crustaceans.

Polar regions: The polar regions of the ocean, near the North and South Poles, are very cold and icy. They are home to animals such as seals, penguins, and polar bears.

Coral reefs are underwater ecosystems formed by colonies of coral. Coral is a type of small, soft-bodied animal that belongs to the class Anthozoa in the phylum Cnidaria. Coral reefs are some of the most diverse and valuable ecosystems on Earth. They provide habitat for a wide variety of plants and animals, including many endangered species. Coral reefs also provide important economic, cultural, and recreational value.

Coral reefs are found in warm, shallow, clear waters, typically in the tropics and subtropics. They are most commonly found in the Pacific and Indian Oceans, as well as the Red Sea and the Caribbean Sea. Coral reefs are formed over thousands of years as coral polyps, which are the individual animals that make up a coral colony, secrete a hard, calcium carbonate skeleton.

As coral polyps die, their skeletons accumulate, forming a structure that provides a foundation for new coral polyps to grow. This process creates a complex and varied habitat that is home to a wide variety of plants and animals.

There are three main types of coral reefs: fringing reefs, barrier reefs, and atolls. Fringing reefs are found close to shore and are directly attached to the land. Barrier reefs are found further offshore and are separated from the shore by a lagoon. Atolls are ring-shaped reefs that enclose a lagoon.

Coral reefs are facing many threats, including climate change, pollution, overfishing, and coastal development. These threats can cause coral reefs to become degraded or destroyed, which can have significant negative impacts on the plants and animals that depend on them, as well as on the people who rely on them for food, income, and protection from storms.

There are many different types of coral reef fish, and they can be classified in several ways. One way to classify coral reef fishes is by their habitat, which can include shallow coral reefs, deep coral reefs, coral lagoons, and coral atolls. Another way to classify coral reef fishes is by their behavior, which can include schooling species, solitary species, and species that form pairs.

Still, another way to classify coral reef fishes is by their size, which can range from small species that are just a few centimeters in length to large species that can grow to over a meter in length. Finally, coral reef fishes can also be classified by their feeding habits, which can include herbivores, carnivores, and omnivores.

# SHALLOW CORAL REEF FISHES

Shallow coral reefs are home to a diverse array of fish species, many of which are brightly colored and visually striking. These reefs are typically found in shallow, warm waters near the surface and are characterized by the presence of coral, which provides a hard substrate for the attachment of algae and other organisms. The shallow waters and the abundance of coral provide a rich habitat for a variety of fish species, including herbivores, carnivores, and omnivores.

Many shallow coral reef fish are herbivores, feeding on algae and other plant matter. Examples of herbivorous coral reef fish include parrotfish, surgeonfish, and rabbitfish. Carnivorous coral reef fish, on the other hand, feed on other animals, including smaller fish, crustaceans, and mollusks. Examples of carnivorous coral reef fish include lionfish, snappers, and groupers. Omnivorous coral reef fish feed on a combination of plant and animal matter. Examples of omnivorous coral reef fish include damselfish and wrasses.

Shallow coral reefs are important ecosystems because they support a wide variety of marine life and are home to many commercially important fish species. They are also important for tourism and recreation, as they are popular destinations for snorkeling and diving. However, shallow coral reefs are vulnerable to a variety of threats, including climate change, overfishing, pollution, and habitat destruction, which can have negative impacts on the fish species that depend on them.

## DEEP CORAL REEFS

Deep coral reefs, also known as mesophotic coral reefs, are coral reefs that are found at depths ranging from 30 to 150 meters (about 100 to 500 feet). These reefs are found in both tropical and subtropical regions, and they are characterized by a lower light intensity and a higher water pressure compared to shallow coral reefs.

Unlike shallow coral reefs, which are dominated by coral species that contain symbiotic algae called zooxanthellae, deep coral reefs are often dominated by coral species that do not contain zooxanthellae. These corals rely on other sources of energy, such as detritus and dissolved organic matter, to survive.

Deep coral reefs are home to a diverse array of marine life, including many species that are found nowhere else on Earth. These reefs are also important for the health of shallow coral reefs, as they provide a source of larvae for shallow reefs.

Despite their importance, deep coral reefs are not as well studied as shallow coral reefs, and there is still much that scientists do not know about them. However, they are increasingly being recognized as important ecosystems that deserve greater protection.

## DEEP CORAL REEF FISHES

Deep coral reefs, these reefs are home to a variety of fish species that have adapted to living in the lower light levels found at these depths. Some examples of fish species that may be found on deep coral reefs include snappers, groupers, wrasses, and eels. Many of these species are important economically as they are caught and sold for food.

Some deep coral reef fish species, such as the orangeback basslet, are also popular in the aquarium trade. These fish are adapted to living at depths where light levels are much lower than those found on shallow reefs, and they may have specialized adaptations such as large eyes or bioluminescent organs to help them navigate and locate prey in these dim environments.

# Coral Lagoons

Coral lagoons are shallow areas of water that are surrounded by coral reefs. These ecosystems are home to a diverse range of marine animals, including fish, invertebrates, and marine mammals.

Some of the most common creatures found in coral lagoons include:

Fish: Coral lagoons are home to a wide variety of fish, including tropical species such as parrotfish, angelfish, and groupers. These fish are often brightly colored and are known for their striking patterns and markings.

Marine mammals: Coral lagoons are also home to a variety of marine mammals, including dolphins, whales, and manatees. These animals often feed on the fish and invertebrates that live in the lagoons.

Coral lagoons are important ecosystems because they provide habitat and food for many different species of marine animals. They also play a vital role in the overall health of the coral reef ecosystem, as they help to maintain the balance of species in the area.

Invertebrates: Invertebrates, or animals without a backbone, are also common on coral reefs. Examples include crustaceans like crabs and lobsters, mollusks like snails and clams, and echinoderms like sea urchins and starfish. Many invertebrates have hard exoskeletons and play important roles in the reef ecosystem, such as filtering water and breaking down organic matter.

Algae: Algae are a type of plant that live in the water and provide food and oxygen for other coral reef animals. Many different types of algae live on coral reefs, including macroalgae, which are large and visible to the naked eye, and microalgae, which are small and can only be seen under a microscope. Algae are important because they provide a food source for other animals and help to maintain the health of the coral reef ecosystem.

## MARINE ANIMALS AT REEFS

Coral reefs are home to a diverse array of marine life, including many types of fish, mollusks, crustaceans, and other invertebrates. Some examples of animals that live on or around coral reefs include:

Fish: Many different types of fish live on coral reefs, including butterflyfish, angelfish, clownfish (made famous by the movie "Finding Nemo"), parrotfish, and many others. These fish are often brightly colored and play important roles in the coral reef ecosystem, such as controlling algae growth and helping to maintain the coral.

Mollusks: Mollusks such as snails, clams, and oysters are common on coral reefs.

Crustaceans: Crustaceans such as crabs, lobsters, and shrimp can be found on coral reefs.

Invertebrates: Invertebrates such as sea urchins, sea cucumbers, and sea anemones are also found on coral reefs.

Coral: Coral itself is a living organism, and it is the foundation of the coral reef ecosystem. Coral reefs are formed by the skeletons of coral polyps, which are small, soft-bodied animals that secrete a hard, protective exoskeleton made of calcium carbonate.

Marine mammals: Some marine mammals, such as dolphins and whales, may be found near coral reefs, although they do not typically live on the reefs themselves.

Coral reefs are home to a wide variety of animals, including fish, invertebrates, and algae. Here is a brief overview of some common coral reef animals:

## ESTUARIES

An estuary is a partially enclosed coastal body of water with one or more rivers or streams flowing into it and with a free connection to the open sea. Estuaries are found where the mouth of a river meets the ocean, and are characterized by the mixing of fresh water from the river with salt water from the ocean. This mixing of fresh and saltwater creates a unique and diverse habitat for a wide range of plants and animals, including many species of fish, birds, and other wildlife.

Estuaries are important habitats because they provide a home for many species of animals, and they also serve as nurseries for many types of fish and other marine life. Estuaries are also important because they can help to protect coastlines from erosion and storm surges, and they can provide opportunities for recreation and tourism.

# CHAPTER 3

## DEEP SEA CREATURES AND THE PELAGIC

The deep sea is one of the most mysterious and least understood environments on Earth. Located in the depths of the oceans, below about 200 meters (660 feet), the deep sea is a world of perpetual darkness and extreme pressures. Despite these challenges, the deep sea is home to an incredible array of bizarre and fascinating creatures. Here are just a few examples of the amazing deep sea creatures that have been discovered:

The anglerfish is perhaps one of the most iconic and bizarre deep sea creatures. Found at depths of up to 7,000 meters (23,000 feet), anglerfish are known for their unique method of hunting. They have a glowing lure on the top of their head, which they use to attract prey. When an unsuspecting fish comes close, the anglerfish opens its enormous mouth and sucks in its prey whole.

## ANGLERFISH

Anglerfish are a type of fish that are known for their distinctive method of prey capture, which involves using a modified fin on their head (called the esca or illicium) as a "fishing lure." The esca is typically elongated and can be moved in a way that mimics the movements of small animals, attracting other fish that the anglerfish can then catch and eat. There are many different species of anglerfish, and they can be found in a variety of different habitats, including the deep sea, coral reefs, and shallow coastal waters. Anglerfish are typically small, ranging in size from a few inches to about three feet in length, and they have a variety of different physical characteristics depending on the species.

One of the most distinctive features of anglerfish is their mouth, which is usually very large and full of sharp teeth. This allows them to easily catch and eat a wide variety of prey, including small fish, crustaceans, and cephalopods. Some species of anglerfish also have bioluminescent esca, which they use to attract prey in the dark depths of the ocean.

In addition to their unique method of hunting, anglerfish are also known for their unusual reproductive habits. Many species of anglerfish are sexually dimorphic, meaning that males and females look different from one another. In some species, males are much smaller than females and have a hard time finding a mate. As a result, they will often latch onto a female and fuse with her body, becoming essentially a permanent parasitic mate.

The male will then provide the female with sperm when she is ready to reproduce, while the female provides the male with nourishment. Anglerfish are fascinating creatures that have adapted to survive and thrive in some of the most extreme environments on Earth.

## VIPERFISH

The viperfish is another fearsome predator of the deep sea. Found at depths of up to 1,800 meters (6,000 feet), viperfish are known for their long, sharp teeth and their ability to swim vertically. They use this ability to ambush their prey, which they then impale with their teeth.

The viperfish (also known as Chauliodus Sloane) is a species of marine fish that is known for its long, slender body and large teeth. It is typically found in deep, tropical waters, at depths ranging from 1000 to 4000 feet (300 to 1200 meters). Viperfish are carnivorous, and they feed on smaller fish and crustaceans.

One of the most distinctive features of the viperfish is its large, fang-like teeth, which are used to grasp and hold onto prey. These teeth are angled backward, which helps to prevent the prey from escaping. Viperfish also have long, thin body that is adapted for life in the deep ocean. They have small, slender heads, and their eyes are located on the tops of their heads, which allows them to see prey above them in the water column.

In addition to their large teeth and elongated bodies, viperfish are also known for their bioluminescent capabilities. They have photophores (light-producing organs) on their bodies that allow them to emit soft blue-green light. It is believed that this light is used for communication and attracting prey.

Despite their fearsome appearance and predatory behavior, viperfish are relatively small, with adult individuals typically reaching lengths of only about 20-30 cm (8-12 inches). They are not considered to be a threat to humans, and they are not fished commercially.

# GIANT TUBE WORM

The giant tube worm is a bizarre and little-known deep sea creature. Found at depths of up to 8,000 meters (26,000 feet), these worms can grow up to 3 meters (10 feet) in length. They have a unique ability to survive in the extreme conditions of the deep sea, thanks to a symbiotic relationship with bacteria that live inside their bodies. These bacteria provide the worms with energy, while the worms provide the bacteria with a safe and nutritious environment.

The giant tube worm (Riftia pachyptila) is a species of tube worm that is known for its ability to thrive in extreme environments, such as those found near hydrothermal vents on the seafloor. These worms are found in the Pacific Ocean and are characterized by their bright red plumes, which are used for respiration and exchange of gases.

One of the most notable features of the giant tube worm is its ability to survive in an environment that is completely devoid of sunlight and contains no photosynthetic organisms. Instead, the worms rely on chemosynthesis to obtain energy, using bacteria that are present in their plumes to convert chemicals, such as hydrogen sulfide, into usable energy.

The giant tube worm has a complex anatomy, with a long, slender body that is divided into three main regions: the head, the trunk, and the tail. The head of the worm is equipped with a mouth and a prostomial lobe, which is used for respiration and exchange of gasses. The trunk of the worm is made up of segmented segments called chaetigers, which contain the worm's reproductive organs and gills. The tail of the worm, known as the pygidium, is used for anchoring the worm to the seafloor.

Overall, the giant tube worm is an interesting and unique organism that can thrive in some of the most extreme environments on Earth.

## DEEP SEA DRAGONFISH

The deep sea dragonfish is a small but ferocious predator of the deep sea. Found at depths of up to 3,000 meters (10,000 feet), these fish have sharp teeth and long, barbed fins that they use to catch their prey. They also have a unique ability to produce their own light, using bioluminescent organs on their body.

The deep sea dragonfish (also known as the Stomiidae) is a family of small, ferocious predatory fish that live in the deep sea. They are found in all the world's oceans, at depths ranging from 200 to 4,500 meters (660 to

14,760 feet). One of the most distinctive features of the deep sea dragonfish is its long, needle-like teeth, which it uses to catch and eat other small fish and invertebrates.

Dragonfish have several adaptations that allow them to survive in the deep sea, where light is scarce and temperatures are cold. They have large eyes that are sensitive to low levels of light, which helps them to locate prey in the dark. They also have long, slender bodies and small scales, which make them more hydrodynamic and allow them to swim quickly and efficiently.

Dragonfish are carnivorous and predatory and will eat almost anything they can catch. They have a varied diet that includes small fish, squid, and other invertebrates. Some species of dragonfish also have photophores, which are light-emitting organs that they use to attract prey.

There are several different species of deep-sea dragonfish, including the barbed dragonfish, the longfin dragonfish, and the black dragonfish. These fish are typically between 5 and 30 centimeters (2 and 12 inches) in length, although some species can grow up to 50 centimeters (20 inches). Despite their small size, dragonfish are formidable predators that play an important role in the deep sea ecosystem.

# DEEP SEA OCTOPUS

The deep sea octopus is a mysterious and little-known creature that dwells in the depths of the ocean. Found at depths of up to 7,000 meters (23,000 feet), these octopuses are adapted to the extreme pressures and cold temperatures of the deep sea. They have a unique anatomy, with long tentacles and a small, compact body.

The deep sea octopus, also known as the "bathypelagic octopus," is a species of octopus that lives in the deep sea at depths of between 200 and 1000 meters (656 and 3281 feet). These octopuses are adapted to living in the extreme conditions of the deep sea, where there is little light and the pressure is much higher than at the surface.

One adaptation that deep sea octopuses have is that they have large, highly developed eyes that are sensitive to low levels of light. This allows them to see the dimly lit depths of the ocean. They also can change the color and pattern of their skin, which helps them to blend in with their surroundings and avoid predators.

Deep sea octopuses have several other adaptations that allow them to survive in the deep sea. For example, they have a highly developed nervous system that allows them to respond quickly to stimuli, and they have a complex network of blood vessels that helps to regulate their body temperature and oxygen levels. They are also able to move quickly through the water using their jet propulsion system, which allows them to escape from predators or catch prey.

Despite these adaptations, life in the deep sea is still challenging for the deep sea octopus. They have to contend with a lack of food and extreme pressure, and they have a shorter lifespan than octopuses that live in shallower waters. However, they can survive and thrive in these challenging conditions thanks to their impressive array of adaptations.

These are just a few examples of the amazing and bizarre creatures that inhabit the deep sea. Despite our advances in technology and our increasing knowledge of the oceans, there is still much we have yet to learn about this mysterious and fascinating world.

## PELAGIC OPEN WATER ANIMALS

Pelagic animals are adapted to living in the vast, open water of the ocean, where they must be able to find food and avoid predators. Many pelagic animals are highly mobile and can swim long distances in search of food. They may also have specialized physical adaptations, such as streamlined bodies or sharp teeth, that help them hunt and defend themselves in the open water.

Pelagic animals are those that inhabit the open water of the ocean, rather than the sea floor or the coasts. This includes a wide variety of animals, from small plankton and krill to larger fish, sea birds, and marine mammals. Some examples of pelagic animals include:

Fish: Tuna, mackerel, and are all examples of pelagic fish that spend most of their lives in the open ocean.

## TUNA

Tuna is a type of saltwater fish that belongs to the family Scombridae, which also includes mackerel and bonito. There are many different species of tuna, ranging in size and color, but they are all characterized by their streamlined bodies, which are adapted for fast swimming and allow them to pursue their prey over long distances.

Tuna are found in all the world's oceans and are typically found in the open water, far from shore. They are highly migratory, moving long distances to follow their prey and reproduce. Some species of tuna can swim at speeds of up to 70 miles per hour, making them some of the fastest fish in the sea.

Tuna are predatory fish and feed on a variety of other marine organisms, including smaller fish, squid, and crustaceans. They have a unique ability to maintain their body temperature at a higher level than the surrounding water, which allows them to tolerate colder water and pursue their prey in a wider range of environments.

Tuna is an important food source for both humans and other animals. They are caught using a variety of methods, including pole and line, purse seine, and longline fishing. Tuna are also farmed in some parts of the world, although this is less common than wild capture.

## Mackerel Fish

Mackerel is a type of fish that is found in the open waters of the world's oceans. It is a slender, fast-swimming fish that is adapted to life in the open sea. Some of the adaptations that enable mackerel to thrive in open water include:

Streamlined body shape: Mackerels have a slim, streamlined body shape that allows them to swim quickly and efficiently through the water. This shape also reduces drag and makes it easier for the fish to move through the water, even in choppy or turbulent conditions.

Strong swim bladder: Mackerels have a large swim bladder, which is an internal organ that helps them maintain buoyancy in the water. The swim bladder is filled with gases that can be adjusted to help the fish rise or sink in the water column. This is an important adaptation for a fish that lives in the open water, where there may be few landmarks or points of reference.

Fast swimming speed: Mackerel are fast swimmers and can reach speeds of up to 40 miles per hour. This speed helps them evade predators and capture prey in the open water.

Strong eyesight: Mackerels have excellent eyesight, which helps them locate prey and avoid predators in the open water. Their eyes are positioned on the sides of their head, giving them a wide field of vision.

Specialized scales: Mackerels have small, smooth scales that overlap like tiles on a roof. These scales help the fish move through the water with minimal resistance and reduce drag.

Camouflage: Mackerel have a metallic sheen on their bodies that helps them blend in with the surrounding water. This camouflage helps them avoid being seen by predators and enables them to sneak up on prey.

## MARLIN

Marlins are adapted for life in the open water of the tropical and subtropical oceans. They are known for their sleek, streamlined bodies and long, pointed bills, which they use to slash at their prey. Marlin are also fast swimmers, able to reach speeds of up to 80 km/h (50 mph) when attacking prey or evading predators.

One of the most distinctive features of marlin is their elongated upper jaw, which extends into a long, pointed bill. This bill is used as a weapon to stun or kill prey, as well as to defend against predators. Marlin also has several other adaptations that help them survive in the open ocean, including:

A streamlined body: Marlins have a sleek, hydrodynamic body shape that allows them to swim quickly and efficiently through the water.

Large, powerful fins: Marlins have large, powerful pectoral fins that they use to steer and stabilize themselves while swimming. They also have a large, triangular dorsal fin that runs along their back, as well as a small anal fin and a pair of elongated pelvic fins.

Strong muscles: Marlins have large, powerful muscles that allow them to swim at high speeds and make sharp turns.

Good eyesight: Marlins have excellent eyesight and can spot prey from a distance. They also have specialized cells in their eyes called chromatophores, which allow them to see in low-light conditions.

Marlin are well-adapted to life in the open water, where they use their speed, agility, and powerful bill to hunt and defend themselves against predators.

# SEA BIRD

Sea birds: Albatross, petrels, and shearwaters are all pelagic birds that feed on fish and other marine life found in the open water.

## Albatross

Albatrosses are a group of seabirds that are known for their long wingspans, which can reach up to 11 feet in some species. They are found in many parts of the world, including the Southern Ocean and the North Pacific. Albatrosses are adapted to life at sea and have many features that enable them to thrive in this environment.

One important feature of albatrosses is their beak, which is long, thin, and curved. This shape allows them to easily catch and eat small fish and other marine animals, such as squid and krill. Albatrosses are also skilled at fishing using a technique called "dynamic soaring," in which they use the wind to gain altitude and then glide over long distances in search of food.

In addition to their physical adaptations, albatrosses also have a number of behavioral traits that help them survive in the open ocean. For example, they are known for their long-distance migrations, which can take them across entire ocean basins. Albatrosses are also highly social birds and often form large colonies on remote islands.

The features and behaviors of albatrosses are well-suited to their role as open-water birds, enabling them to thrive in the challenging marine environment.

**Petrels**

Petrels are a group of seabirds that belong to the family Procellariidae. They are known for their long, narrow wings and their ability to fly long distances over open water. Many species of petrels are adapted to life at sea and can be found all over the world's oceans.

Petrels are generally small to medium-sized birds, with most species weighing between 4 and 16 ounces. They have a streamlined body shape and long wings that allow them to soar over the ocean for extended periods of time. Most petrels have a dark plumage, which helps to camouflage them against the dark water below.

One of the most distinctive features of petrels is their long, pointed bill, which is used for picking small fish and invertebrates out of the water. Some species of petrels also have a hooked tip on their bill, which helps them to grab onto prey more effectively.

Petrels are primarily found in the Southern Hemisphere, and many species breed on remote islands where they are free from predation. Some petrels, such as the albatross, are known for their long migrations, which can take them across entire ocean basins.

Petrels are an important part of the marine ecosystem, and many species are considered indicators of the health of the oceans. However, some petrel species are endangered due to habitat loss, overfishing, and other human activities, and conservation efforts are underway to protect these birds and their habitats.

## Shearwater Seabird

Shearwaters are a type of seabird that belong to the Procellariidae family, which also includes petrels and albatrosses. They are found in all the world's oceans, and many species have wide ranges that allow them to breed on islands and coastal areas in various parts of the world.

Shearwaters are adapted for life at sea, with long, narrow wings that allow them to efficiently glide over long distances. They typically feed on small fish, squid, and other marine animals, which they hunt by diving into the water from the air. Shearwaters are known for their ability to "shear" the water's surface with their wings, hence their name.

Some species of shearwaters, such as the common shearwater and the great shearwater, are migratory, traveling long distances between their breeding and non-breeding grounds. During the breeding season, shearwaters nest in burrows or on the ground, laying a single egg that both parents help incubate.

Shearwaters are important indicators of the health of marine ecosystems, as their diet and breeding habits are closely tied to the availability of food in the oceans.

## Marine mammals

Marine mammals: Whales, dolphins, and porpoises are all pelagic mammals that live and feed in the open ocean.

### Whale

Whales are a group of marine mammals that belong to the order Cetacea. They are some of the largest animals on Earth and can be found in all of the world's oceans. There are two main types of whales: toothed whales and baleen whales. Toothed whales, such as sperm whales and killer whales, have teeth and are carnivorous. They use their teeth to hunt fish, squid, and other marine animals. Baleen whales, such as blue whales and humpback whales, have baleen plates instead of teeth. They filter their food (small crustaceans called krill) from seawater using their baleen plates.

Whales are known for their distinctive vocalizations, which they use to communicate with one another. They are also intelligent animals that have been observed exhibiting complex social behaviors and problem-solving abilities. Some species of whales, such as killer whales and bottlenose dolphins, are even known to use tools.

Whales are among the largest animals on Earth, and their size can vary greatly depending on the species. Some species of whales, such as the blue whale, are the largest animals ever to have lived on Earth, while others, such as the dwarf sperm whale, are much smaller.

The blue whale is the largest known species of whale, and it can grow up to 100 feet (30 meters) in length and can weigh as much as 200 tons. Other large species of whales include the fin whale, which can grow up to 85 feet (26 meters) in length, and the humpback whale, which can grow up to 52 feet (16 meters) in length.

On the other hand, smaller species of whales, such as the dwarf sperm whale, can grow to just about 10 feet (3 meters) in length and weigh only about 1 ton.

The size of a whale can vary greatly depending on the species, with some whales being much larger than others.

## Dolphins

Dolphins are a type of marine mammal that belongs to the family Delphinidae. They are known for their playful behavior, intelligence, and streamlined bodies, which allow them to be fast swimmers.

Dolphins are found in many different parts of the world, including the coastal waters of many countries and in the open ocean. They are carnivores and feed on a variety of prey, including fish, squid, and crustaceans.

Unlike whales, which are also marine mammals, dolphins are generally smaller and have a more streamlined, streamlined body shape. They also have a distinctively shaped head, with a beak-like snout and a blowhole on top of their head for breathing.

Dolphins are social animals and are often seen in groups, or pods, which can range in size from just a few individuals to several hundred. They use a variety of vocalizations and body language to communicate with each other and are also able to use echolocation to navigate and locate prey.

Dolphins are popular with humans and are often kept in captivity for entertainment purposes. However, there is an ongoing debate about the ethics of keeping these intelligent and social animals in captivity.

### Porpoises

Porpoises are a group of small, toothed whales that are closely related to dolphins. They are found in coastal and open waters throughout the world and are known for their streamlined bodies and sharp, conical teeth. Porpoises are generally smaller than dolphins, with shorter beaks and rounder bodies. They are also generally less vocal and more elusive than dolphins, making them more difficult to observe in the wild.

Like dolphins, porpoises are intelligent and highly social animals that communicate with each other through a variety of vocalizations and body language. They are also skilled hunters, using their sonar abilities to locate prey in the water. Porpoises feed on a variety of small fish, squid, and crustaceans, and are known to hunt cooperatively in groups.

There are six species of porpoises, including the harbor porpoise, Dall's porpoise, and the vaquita, which is the most endangered species of porpoise. Porpoises are threatened by a variety of human activities, including pollution, overfishing, and habitat destruction. They are also at risk of accidental entanglement in fishing gear and collisions with boats.

# CHAPTER 4

## COASTAL ESTUARINE ANIMAL

Coastal and estuarine animals are animals that live in or near the coast and in estuaries, which are bodies of water where freshwater from rivers mixes with saltwater from the ocean. These animals are adapted to live in the unique and changing conditions found in these environments, which can vary greatly depending on factors such as tides, temperature, and salinity.

There is a diverse range of coastal and estuarine animals, including many species of fish, birds, and invertebrates. Some common examples include salmon, which migrate from the ocean to spawn in freshwater rivers and streams; seabirds such as gulls and terns, which feed on fish and other marine life; and crabs and lobsters, which can be found in shallow coastal waters and estuaries.

In addition to these more well-known animals, there are many other species that are adapted to live in coastal and estuarine environments. For example, mangroves are trees that grow in the tidal zones of tropical and subtropical coastlines and are adapted to tolerate saltwater and high levels of humidity. Similarly, salt marshes are wetlands found along the coast that are characterized by salt-tolerant grasses and other plants, and are home to a variety of animals such as insects, amphibians, and birds.

Coastal and estuarine animals play important roles in the ecosystem, and many of them are also economically and culturally important to humans. For example, many species of fish that live in these environments are important sources of food for both people and other animals, and shellfish such as oysters and clams can be harvested for food and other uses. In addition, these animals and their habitats provide important ecosystem services such as water purification, erosion control, and storm protection.

Coastal and estuarine animals are an integral part of the ecosystems in which they live and play important roles in the health and well-being of both humans and the natural world.

# Coastal Estuarine Animal

Here are some examples of animals that can be found in coastal and estuarine environments:

Fish: species such as salmon, halibut, and trout can be found in these environments.

Birds: many bird species, such as pelicans, seagulls, and terns, make their homes in or near coastal and estuarine areas.

Crustaceans: these include animals such as crabs, lobsters, and shrimp, which are often found in these environments.

Mollusks: these include animals such as clams, oysters, and mussels, which can be found in the intertidal zone of these environments.

Reptiles: species such as sea turtles and saltwater crocodiles can be found in these environments.

Mammals: species such as seals, dolphins, and whales can be found in or near these environments.

# Migratory Ocean Animals

Migratory animals of the ocean are animals that move between different areas of the ocean at different times of the year. These migrations are often driven by changes in temperature, food availability, and the need to reproduce. Some examples of migratory animals in the ocean include whales, sharks, sea turtles, and various species of fish.

Whales are perhaps the most well-known migratory animals in the ocean. They migrate to different parts of the world depending on the season, often traveling long distances in search of food and breeding grounds. There are several different species of whales, each with its own unique migration patterns. For example, gray whales migrate from the Arctic to the warm waters of Mexico and back again each year.

Sharks also migrate long distances, often following food sources such as schools of fish or seals. Some species of sharks, such as the great white shark, are known to migrate thousands of miles each year.

Sea turtles are another example of migratory animals in the ocean. They migrate to different parts of the world to breed, with many species returning to the same beach where they were born to lay their eggs. After the eggs hatch, the baby turtles migrate to different parts of the ocean to grow and mature.

Fish also migrate, often moving between different areas of the ocean to follow food sources or to reproduce. Many species of salmon, for example, migrate from the ocean to freshwater rivers and streams to spawn.

## Whale Migration in Ocean

Whale migration is the seasonal movement of whales from one area to another in search of food, breeding grounds, or more favorable conditions. Many species of whales migrate over long distances each year, traveling thousands of kilometers between their feeding and breeding grounds.

There are several theories about why whales migrate. One theory is that whales migrate in search of food. For example, some species of whales migrate from colder polar regions to warmer tropical waters to feed on species of fish and krill that are more abundant there. Other species of whales migrate to areas where certain types of plankton or other small organisms are more prevalent.

Another theory is that whales migrate to breed and give birth. For example, some species of whales migrate to specific areas to mate and bear their young, and then migrate back to their feeding grounds once the offspring are old enough to fend for themselves.

Whale migration patterns can vary greatly depending on the species of whale and the region in which they live. Some whales, such as gray whales and humpback whales, migrate long distances each year, while others, such as killer whales and sperm whales, may not migrate as far or at all.

Scientists study whale migration patterns in order to better understand these animals and to help protect them. Many whale species are threatened or endangered due to a variety of factors, including habitat loss, hunting, and pollution, and understanding their migration patterns can help conservation efforts.

**Migration of the shark in the ocean**

Shark migration is the movement of sharks from one place to another in the ocean. This can be a seasonal migration, in which sharks move to different areas depending on the time of year, or it can be a lifelong migration, in which sharks move to different areas as they grow and mature.

There are several factors that can influence shark migration. One of the most important factors is temperature, as sharks prefer warmer waters. They may migrate to different areas in order to find water that is more suitable for their needs.

Food availability is also a key factor in shark migration. Sharks will migrate to areas where there is an abundance of food, such as areas with high concentrations of fish or other marine life.

Another factor that can influence shark migration is the availability of breeding grounds. Sharks will often migrate to specific areas in order to breed and reproduce and may return to these areas year after year.

Sharks have several different methods of migration, including swimming long distances, using ocean currents, and hitching rides on larger marine animals. Some species of sharks are known to migrate long distances, traveling thousands of miles in a single year.

Shark migration is an important aspect of their biology and helps to ensure the survival of these fascinating and important creatures.

**Migration of the sea turtle in the ocean**

Sea turtles are migratory creatures that spend their entire lives in the ocean, traveling long distances between their feeding grounds and nesting sites.

The specific migration patterns of sea turtles vary depending on the species and location, but most follow a regular cycle of moving between feeding and breeding areas.

For example, the loggerhead sea turtle (Caretta caretta) feeds in the Atlantic and Pacific Oceans, but nests almost exclusively on the coasts of the southeastern United States, the Caribbean, and Mexico. Each year, adult females migrate to their nesting beaches to lay eggs, typically traveling over 1,000 miles (1,600 km).

The green sea turtle (Chelonia mydas) feeds on seagrass and algae in shallow coastal waters, but nests on tropical beaches around the world. Adult females typically return to the same beach where they were born to lay their eggs, traveling hundreds or thousands of miles depending on the location.

Other sea turtle species, such as the hawksbill (Eretmochelys imbricata) and the leatherback (Dermochelys coriacea), have similarly complex migration patterns, with some individuals traveling over 10,000 miles (16,000 km) in a single year.

Despite their impressive endurance, sea turtles face numerous threats during their migrations, including habitat loss, fishing gear entanglement, and climate change. Conservation efforts are ongoing to protect these vulnerable species and ensure their continued survival.

Migratory animals of the ocean play a vital role in the health and balance of marine ecosystems, and their migrations help to ensure the survival and diversity of species throughout the world's oceans.

## Strange and unusual sea creatures

Anglerfish: These deep-sea fish are known for their distinctive lures on their heads, which they use to attract prey. They also have large, toothy jaws and can grow up to three feet in length.

Blobfish: These strange-looking fish are native to the deep waters off the coasts of Australia and Tasmania. They have no bones in their bodies and are able to survive at great depths due to their extremely low density.

Glass squid: These small, transparent squids are found in the deep waters of the Pacific and Atlantic Oceans. They have the ability to light up their bodies, which helps them communicate with other members of their species and attract prey.

Giant tube worms: These worms are found in the deep waters near hydrothermal vents and can grow up to 10 feet in length. They have a bright red plume on the end of their bodies and are able to survive in extreme conditions due to a special type of bacteria that lives inside their cells.

Mola mola: Also known as the "ocean sunfish," the mola is the heaviest bony fish in the world and can weigh up to 5,000 pounds. They are found in tropical and temperate waters around the globe and are known for their distinctive round bodies and large, fin-like dorsal and anal fins.

Blue Ringed Octopus: This small octopus is native to the Pacific and Indian Oceans, and is known for the bright blue rings that appear on its body when it is threatened. It is also highly venomous, and a bite from a blue-ringed octopus can be lethal.

Dumbo Octopus: As its name suggests, this octopus has large, ear-like fins that resemble Dumbo's ears. It is a deep sea dweller and can be found at depths of up to 7,200 feet.

Frilled Shark: This shark is characterized by its long, snake-like body and frilled gills, which it can use to swim backward and escape predators. It is a rare species and is found in the Atlantic and Pacific Oceans.

Goblin Shark: This shark is known for its unusual, elongated snout and sharp, blade-like teeth. It is a deep sea dweller and is rarely seen by humans.

Jellyfish: These gelatinous creatures come in a variety of shapes and sizes, and can be found in every ocean on Earth. Some species, like the lion's mane jellyfish, can grow to be over 100 feet long, while others, like the sea wasp, are highly venomous.

Mantis Shrimp: These colorful crustaceans are known for their distinctive, multi-colored shells and powerful claws, which they use to crush shells and hunt prey. They are found in tropical and subtropical waters around the world.

Nautilus: This cephalopod is known for its distinctive, spiral-shaped shell and tentacles. It is a relative of the octopus and squid and is found in the Pacific and Indian Oceans.

Sea Cucumber: These strange, tube-like creatures are found on the ocean floor and are known for their ability to expel their internal organs as a defense mechanism.

Syngnathidae: This family of fish includes seahorses, pipefish, and the sea dragon. They are known for their unique appearance, with seahorses having a horse-like head and pipefish having a long, thin body.

# CHAPTER 5

## MARINE ANIMALS EXTINCTION RISK

Endangered and threatened sea creatures refer to marine animals that are at risk of extinction due to various factors such as human activities, pollution, overfishing, and climate change. Endangered species are those that are in imminent danger of extinction, while threatened species are those that are likely to become endangered in the near future. Conservation efforts are often put in place to protect these animals and their habitats in order to prevent their extinction.

Endangered and threatened sea creatures include:

Blue Whale (Endangered)

North Atlantic Right Whale (Endangered)

Hawksbill Sea Turtle (Critically Endangered)

Leatherback Sea Turtle (Critically Endangered)

Vaquita (Critically Endangered)

Pacific Ridley Sea Turtle (Endangered)

West Indian Manatee (Endangered)

Hammerhead Shark (Endangered)

Beluga Sturgeon (Endangered)

Many other sea creatures are also endangered or threatened due to human activities such as overfishing, pollution, and climate change. It's important that we take steps to protect these species and their habitats.

The Blue Whale (Balaenoptera musculus) is a species of marine mammal that is currently listed as Endangered by the International Union for Conservation of Nature (IUCN). Blue whales are the largest animals on Earth, growing up to 100 feet in length and weighing as much as 200 tons. They are found in all of the world's oceans but are most commonly found in the Antarctic and Arctic regions. Blue whales feed mainly on krill, a small shrimp-like crustacean, and can consume up to 4 tons of krill per day.

The North Atlantic Right Whale (Eubalaena glacialis) is also a critically endangered species of marine mammal. They are found in the North Atlantic Ocean and have a population size of around 350-400 individuals. These whales are known for their black color, large head, and short, round dorsal fin. They feed on small crustaceans and plankton. The main threats to the North Atlantic right whale are entanglement in fishing gear and ship strikes.

The Hawksbill Sea Turtle (Eretmochelys imbricata) is a species of marine turtle that is currently listed as Critically Endangered by the International Union for Conservation of Nature (IUCN). These turtles are found in tropical and subtropical waters of the Atlantic,

Pacific, and Indian Oceans. They have a distinctive hawk-like beak, which gives them their name, and a pattern of overlapping scales on their shells that creates a unique and colorful pattern.

Hawksbill sea turtles are primarily herbivorous, feeding on sponges, sea anemones, and other invertebrates. They are known for their beautiful shells, which were highly prized for use in decorative items such as combs, brushes, and eyeglass frames. This has led to the over-exploitation of the species, and the hawksbill sea turtle is now considered one of the most endangered sea turtle species in the world. Other threats include pollution, coastal development and loss of nesting beaches, and accidental capture in fishing gear.

**The Leatherback Sea Turtle (Dermochelys coriacea)** is a species of marine turtle that is currently listed as Critically Endangered by the International Union for Conservation of Nature (IUCN). These turtles are found in all the world's oceans but are most commonly found in tropical and subtropical waters. They are the largest sea turtles, growing up to 7 feet in length and weighing as much as 2,000 pounds.

The leatherback sea turtle is unique among sea turtles in that it does not have a hard shell, but instead has a carapace covered in a leathery skin. They are also different from other sea turtles in that they feed primarily on jellyfish and other soft-bodied animals.

Leatherback sea turtles are facing many threats, including over-harvesting of eggs, accidental capture in fishing gear, and loss of nesting beaches due to coastal development. Climate change also plays a role in the reduction of their population as the temperature of the sand on the beach determines the sex of hatchlings and warmer sands produce more females than males. The leatherback sea turtle's population has declined by more than 70% in the last century, and without significant conservation efforts, the species may face extinction.

**The Mediterranean monk seal (Monachus monachus)** is a critically endangered species of seal that is found in the Mediterranean Sea and the northeastern Atlantic Ocean. They are one of the most endangered marine mammals in the world, with only around 600 individuals remaining. The main threats to the Mediterranean monk seal include habitat loss and degradation, accidental capture in fishing gear, and human disturbance. Conservation efforts are currently underway to try and protect and recover this species, including the creation of protected areas and the implementation of measures to reduce bycatch in fishing gear.

**The Vaquita (Phocoena sinus)** is a critically endangered species of porpoise that is found only in the northern Gulf of California, Mexico. It is considered one of the most endangered marine mammals in the world, with an estimated population of only around 30 individuals remaining. The main threats to the Vaquita include accidental entanglement in fishing gear, particularly in gillnets used for catching fish and shrimp, and habitat loss and degradation. Conservation efforts are currently underway to try and protect and recover this species, including a ban on gillnet fishing in the Vaquita's range, increased enforcement of fishing regulations, and the creation of a protected area for the Vaquita.

**The Pacific Ridley Sea turtle (Lepidochelys olivacea),** also known as the Olive Ridley sea turtle, is a species of marine turtle found in warm waters of the Pacific Ocean, particularly in the coastal regions of Mexico, Central America, and South America. They are considered a vulnerable species by IUCN. The main threats to the Pacific Ridley sea turtle include habitat loss and degradation, accidental capture in fishing gear, poaching of eggs and adults, and the destruction of nesting beaches by coastal development and beachfront lighting. Conservation efforts are currently underway to try and protect and recover this species, including the creation of protected areas and the implementation of measures to reduce bycatch in fishing gear.

**The West Indian manatee (Trichechus manatus)** is a large aquatic mammal that is native to the Caribbean and the Gulf of Mexico. It is an endangered species, with an estimated population of around 13,000 individuals. The manatee's primary threats are human activities such as boat strikes, habitat loss, and pollution. Efforts are currently being made to protect and conserve the species through habitat restoration and conservation programs, as well as education and awareness campaigns. The West Indian manatee is protected by law in both the United States and many Caribbean countries.

**Hammerhead sharks** are a group of sharks that belong to the family Sphyrnidae. They are named for their distinctive hammer-shaped head, which is used to locate prey using their electroreceptors.

Several species of hammerhead sharks are considered endangered, including the scalloped hammerhead shark (Sphyrna lewini) and the great hammerhead shark (Sphyrna mokarran). These sharks are threatened by overfishing for their fins, which are highly valued in the shark fin trade. Habitat loss and degradation also contribute to their decline.

Conservation efforts are being made to protect hammerhead sharks, including the implementation of fishing regulations and protected areas. However, more work is needed to ensure the survival of these species.

**The Beluga Sturgeon (Huso huso)** is a species of fish that is native to the Caspian Sea, the Black Sea, and the Azov Sea. It is one of the largest freshwater fish in the world and can grow up to 20 feet in length and weigh over 2,200 pounds. The Beluga Sturgeon is an anadromous fish, which means that it spends most of its life in saltwater but returns to freshwater to spawn.

The Beluga Sturgeon is considered to be critically endangered due to overfishing, habitat loss, and pollution. The population of Beluga Sturgeon has declined dramatically in recent years, with some estimates suggesting that the population has declined by over 90% in the last century. This decline is primarily due to overfishing for caviar, which is considered a delicacy. Habitat loss and pollution in the Caspian Sea, Black Sea, and Azov Sea are also believed to be contributing factors.

Efforts are being made to conserve and protect the Beluga Sturgeon. Several countries, including Russia, Kazakhstan, and Azerbaijan, have implemented laws and regulations to protect the species. Additionally, several organizations are working to restore the population of Beluga Sturgeon through breeding and reintroduction programs.

Human activities have had a significant impact on sea creatures and their habitats.

Pollution, overfishing, and the destruction of coastal habitats are all major threats to marine life. Pollution from plastics and other chemicals harms and kills many sea creatures, and overfishing can lead to the depletion of entire fish populations. Coastal development, such as the building of seawalls and the creation of marinas, can also damage or destroy important habitats, such as coral reefs. To address these issues, conservation efforts have been developed to protect sea creatures and their habitats. These efforts include marine protected areas, where fishing and other activities are restricted to allow fish populations to recover, as well as regulations to limit pollution and protect coastal habitats. Additionally, programs such as sustainable fishing practices, beach cleanups, and public awareness campaigns have been implemented to reduce the impact of human activities on marine life.

Also, research and monitoring programs have been developed to better understand the impacts of human activities on sea creatures and to track the health of marine populations. This information is used to inform conservation and management decisions and to evaluate the effectiveness of conservation efforts.

The conservation of sea creatures and their habitats requires a multifaceted approach, including regulations, education, and research to understand and mitigate the impacts of human activities on the ocean.

Sustainable fishing practices are methods of fishing that aim to preserve fish populations and the overall health of marine ecosystems. These practices include:

Selective harvesting: This involves using fishing gear and techniques that target specific species or sizes of fish, rather than indiscriminately catching all types of fish.

Catch limits: Setting catch limits for different fish species helps to ensure that the population of those species is not overfished.

Habitat protection: Measures such as protecting important spawning or nursery areas help to ensure that fish populations have adequate breeding and feeding grounds.

Bycatch reduction: Bycatch is the unintentional capture of non-target species. Bycatch reduction techniques include using more selective fishing gear, and the release of non-target species that are caught alive.

Monitoring and enforcement: Effective monitoring and enforcement of fishing regulations are important to ensure that sustainable fishing practices are being followed.

Ecosystem-based management: This approach considers the entire ecosystem when making decisions about fishing, rather than just focusing on individual fish populations. This helps to ensure that the overall health of the ecosystem is maintained.

These are just a few examples of sustainable fishing practices. Overall, the goal of sustainable fishing is to allow for the continued harvest of fish while also preserving the health and biodiversity of marine ecosystems.

Marine protected areas (MPAs) are designated regions of the ocean where human activities such as fishing, mining, and oil and gas exploration are restricted in order to protect marine biodiversity and ecosystem health. These areas can range in size from small, localized zones to large, multi-use regions that span entire ocean basins. MPAs can be divided into different types, such as no-take reserves where all extractive activities are prohibited, and multiple-use MPAs where some activities are allowed. The effectiveness of MPAs in protecting marine life and habitats varies depending on a number of factors, including the size and location of the MPA, the level of enforcement, and the specific activities that are restricted.

Overall, MPAs are considered to be an important tool for protecting marine biodiversity and promoting sustainable use of the ocean's resources.

# Beach Cleanup Benefits Ocean Creatures

Beach cleanups can benefit endangered sea creatures in a number of ways. One of the main benefits is that they remove trash and debris from the beach and ocean, which can help to prevent the animals from becoming entangled or ingesting harmful materials. Additionally, beach cleanups can help to protect vital habitats for sea creatures, such as coral reefs and sea grass beds, by removing debris that can damage these areas.

Beach cleanups can also help to reduce the amount of plastic pollution in the ocean, which can have a major impact on sea creatures. Plastic pollution can harm or kill marine animals through entanglement, suffocation, or ingestion. Beach cleanups can also raise awareness about the importance of protecting sea creatures and the ocean, which can lead to additional conservation efforts.

## Fun Ocean Creature Facts

Some interesting facts about sea creatures that might be interesting and fun to know:

1. The blue whale is the largest animal on Earth, and its tongue alone can weigh as much as an elephant.
2. The giant squid can grow up to 43 feet in length and is believed to be the largest invertebrate on Earth.
3. The octopus has three hearts and can change color to camouflage itself.
4. The seahorse is the only animal in the world where the male carries the eggs and gives birth to the young.
5. The starfish can regenerate lost arms, and in some cases, a single arm can grow into a whole new starfish.
6. The great white shark can swim at speeds of up to 25 miles per hour.
7. The electric eel can produce a powerful electric shock that can stun prey or defend itself against predators.
8. The narwhal's tusk is actually an elongated tooth that can grow up to 8 feet long.
9. The clownfish has a symbiotic relationship with anemones, which protect the clownfish from predators.
10. The sea otter has the densest fur of any mammal, with up to one million hairs per square inch.
11. The deepest fish ever found is the Mariana snailfish, which lives at depths of up to 8,178 meters (26,800 feet) in the Mariana Trench.

12. The giant squid, which can reach up to 43 feet in length, is the largest known invertebrate.

13. The vampire squid, which lives in the deep sea, has the ability to turn itself inside out as a defense mechanism.

14. The Anglerfish, which lives in the deep sea, has a bioluminescent "lure" on its head that it uses to attract prey.

15. The deep sea dragonfish has needle-like teeth and photophores (light-emitting organs) along its body.

16. The deep sea hatchet fish has a flattened body and large eyes that allow it to see above it in the dark waters.

17. The deep sea bristlemouth is the most common fish in the ocean.

18. The deep sea fangtooth fish has the largest teeth relative to the body size of any fish in the ocean.

19. Some whales, such as humpbacks, are known for their complex songs, which can last for up to 20 minutes and be heard up to 1,000 miles away.

20. Whales have a unique way of breathing, they have to come to the surface to take a breath, instead of breathing automatically like fish.

21. Some species of whale, such as killer and humpback, are known for their acrobatic displays, including breaching and tail slapping.

22. Whales have a very good sense of hearing and use echolocation to navigate and hunt for food.
23. Whales are long-lived animals, with some species living for over a century.
24. Sharks have been around for over 400 million years, making them one of the oldest species on Earth.
25. The largest shark is the whale shark, which can grow up to 40 feet long and weigh over 20,000 pounds.
26. Sharks can be found in every ocean on Earth.
27. Sharks have a unique skeletal system made of cartilage instead of bone, which makes them more flexible and able to swim faster.
28. Some sharks can swim at speeds of up to 60 miles per hour.
29. Sharks have a highly developed sense of smell, which they use to locate prey from great distances.
30. Sharks are cold-blooded animals, which means their body temperature is regulated by the surrounding water.
31. Albatrosses have the largest wingspan of any bird, spanning up to 11 feet (3.4 meters).
32. Penguins are flightless birds that are excellent swimmers, using their wings as flippers.

33. Frigatebirds are known for their "pirate" behavior - they steal food from other seabirds in mid-air.
34. The Atlantic Puffin's colorful beak fades in winter and becomes more vibrant during the breeding season.
35. Gulls are highly adaptable and can be found in a wide range of environments, from coastlines to cities.
36. Petrels are expert long-distance flyers, often covering thousands of miles during migration.
37. Shearwaters have a unique way of feeding called "shearing," gliding along the water's surface to catch prey.
38. Cormorants are excellent divers, using their webbed feet to propel themselves underwater in search of fish.
39. Pelicans use their expandable throat pouch to catch fish, then drain the water before swallowing the prey.
40. The Blue-footed Booby's name comes from its vibrant blue feet, which play a role in courtship displays.
41. Gannets are known for their dramatic high-speed dives from great heights to catch fish.
42. Manx Shearwaters are known for their eerie calls, which were once believed to be the sounds of lost souls.
43. Oystercatchers have specially adapted bills for prying open shellfish.

44. Terns are agile fliers and can hover in place before diving into the water to catch small fish.

45. The Arctic Tern holds the record for the longest migratory journey, traveling between the Arctic and Antarctic.

46. Puffins are often called "sea parrots" due to their colorful beaks and upright posture.

47. Boobies are skilled plunge-divers, using their streamlined bodies to pierce the water's surface.

48. Albatrosses are known for their elegant gliding flights, using air currents to stay aloft for hours.

49. Storm Petrels are named for their ability to seemingly "dance" on the water's surface during feeding.

50. The Northern Fulmar has a specialized gland that helps it expel a foul-smelling oil when threatened.

51. Jaegers are agile predators that steal food from other seabirds or catch flying insects in mid-air.

52. Puffins can carry a large number of fish in their bills, allowing them to bring food back to their nests.

53. Skuas are known for their aggressive behavior, often harassing other birds to steal their food.

54. Wandering Albatrosses are known for their stunning courtship displays involving synchronized dancing.

55. Shearwaters can be incredibly long-lived, with some individuals known to have lived for over 50 years.

56. Tropicbirds have long tail feathers and are known for their graceful, soaring flights.

57. Penguins have specialized feathers that help keep them insulated and waterproof while swimming.

58. The Arctic Tern's migratory route takes it across the entire globe, covering about 44,000 miles (71,000 kilometers) annually.

59. Skimmers have lower mandibles that are longer than their upper mandibles, allowing them to skim the water's surface for food.

60. Puffins have a distinctive way of holding multiple fish in their bills, allowing them to catch several at once.

61. Phytoplankton, tiny photosynthetic organisms, produce over 50% of Earth's oxygen.

62. Zooplankton, microscopic animals, play a vital role in marine food chains.

63. Diatoms, a type of algae, have intricate silica cell walls with stunning geometric patterns.

64. Bioluminescent plankton lights up the ocean when disturbed, creating mesmerizing displays.

65. Prochlorococcus is the world's smallest and most abundant photosynthetic organism.

66. Jellyfish are considered plankton when in their early stages of life.

67. Some microorganisms can survive extreme conditions like hydrothermal vents and icy polar waters.

68. Bacteriophages are viruses that infect bacteria and are abundant in marine environments.

69. Viruses in the ocean, collectively known as the "virosphere," are crucial in regulating marine ecosystems.

70. Coral reefs rely on symbiotic microorganisms to thrive and provide habitat.

71. Dinoflagellates are responsible for harmful algal blooms, releasing toxins harmful to marine life.

72. The blue color of the ocean is partly due to the absorption and scattering of sunlight by water molecules.

73. Some microorganisms can photosynthesize using infrared light, an adaptation to deeper waters.

74. Planktonic larvae of various marine species often travel great distances on ocean currents.

75. Coccolithophores, algae with calcium carbonate scales, contribute to marine carbon cycling.

76. Archaea are ancient microorganisms that thrive in extreme conditions, like hydrothermal vents.
77. Ocean microbes recycle nutrients, helping to regulate global nutrient cycles.
78. Microbes break down organic matter, playing a crucial role in carbon sequestration.
79. Some microorganisms produce biofluorescence, emitting colorful light under ultraviolet light.
80. Ocean viruses outnumber bacteria by a factor of 10:1.
81. Microbes are used in biotechnology for various applications, including biofuel production.
82. Microbial mats, often found near hydrothermal vents, create unique ecosystems.
83. The "great oxygenation event" was caused by cyanobacteria producing oxygen through photosynthesis.
84. Some microorganisms have antifreeze proteins, allowing them to survive in cold waters.
85. Viruses can transfer genetic material between different marine species.
86. Deep-sea microbes are being investigated for their potential in producing new antibiotics.

87. Some microorganisms can produce their own light, known as bioluminescence, for communication.

88. Microbes help maintain the nitrogen balance in the ocean through processes like denitrification.

89. Iron-oxidizing bacteria play a role in the formation of underwater iron-rich structures.

90. Microorganisms can help break down oil spills, aiding in environmental recovery.

91. Antarctic krill, a vital marine food source, primarily feed on phytoplankton.

92. Some microorganisms can remain dormant for extended periods, waiting for favorable conditions.

93. Cyanobacteria blooms can create "red tide," leading to oxygen depletion and fish kills.

94. Microbes play a role in the degradation of plastic waste in the ocean.

95. Some marine microorganisms exhibit bioluminescence as a defense mechanism against predators.

96. Microbes help produce dimethyl sulfide, which contributes to cloud formation and weather patterns.

97. Sponges and other filter-feeding organisms rely on microorganisms for their diet.

98. Deep-sea hydrothermal vent ecosystems host unique microbial communities.

99. Microorganisms help in the breakdown of dead marine animals, recycling nutrients.

100. The "oceanic carbon pump" involves the sinking of organic matter, driven by microbial processes.

101. Prokaryotes, such as bacteria, were some of the earliest forms of life in the oceans.

102. Some microorganisms produce compounds that have potential medicinal uses.

103. Microbes in the gut of marine animals assist in digestion and nutrient absorption.

104. Harmful algal blooms can produce neurotoxins that impact marine mammals and humans.

105. Microbial diversity in the ocean remains largely unexplored, holding potential for new discoveries.

106. Archaea in extreme environments are often used as analogs for potential extraterrestrial life.

107. Microorganisms contribute to the formation of sediment on the ocean floor.

108. Some microorganisms can fix nitrogen from the atmosphere, enriching marine ecosystems.

109. Ocean microbes play a role in regulating greenhouse gas emissions and global climate.

110. Marine microorganisms continuously adapt to changing environmental conditions for survival.

## Ocean Creature Glossary Terms

1. Plankton: Tiny plants and animals that float in the ocean. They form the base of the ocean food web.
2. Nekton: Swimming animals, such as fish and dolphins, that can move independently of ocean currents.
3. Benthos: Creatures that live on or near the ocean floor, such as crabs and clams.
4. Pelagic: Creatures that live in the open ocean, such as sharks and whales.
5. Cephalopod: A group of marine animals that includes octopus, squid, and cuttlefish. They are known for their intelligence and advanced nervous systems.
6. Echinoderm: A group of marine animals that includes starfish, sea urchins, and sea cucumbers. They are characterized by their radial symmetry and spiny skin.
7. Mollusk: A group of marine animals that includes snails, clams, and squids. They are characterized by their soft bodies and often have a protective shell.
8. Crustaceans: A group of marine animals that includes crabs, lobsters, and shrimp.

They are characterized by their hard exoskeleton and segmented bodies.

9. Coral: a marine invertebrate that forms a hard skeleton and lives in colonies.
10. Polyp: the individual organism that makes up a coral colony.
11. Zooxanthellae: single-celled algae that live symbiotically within coral polyps, providing them with energy through photosynthesis.
12. Anemone: a marine invertebrate that is related to coral and has a similar appearance.
13. Sponge: a simple, sessile animal that filters water for food.
14. Mollusk: a phylum of animals that includes snails, clams, and squids.
15. Crustaceans: a group of animals that includes crabs, shrimp, and lobsters.
16. Fish: a diverse group of aquatic animals that can be found in coral reefs.
17. Anglerfish: a deep-sea fish that has a bioluminescent "lure" on its head to attract prey.
18. Chimaera: a group of deep-sea fish that have a distinctive spine above their eyes.
19. Deep-sea gigantism: a phenomenon where deep-sea animals are much larger than their shallow-water counterparts.
20. Dumbo octopus: a deep-sea octopus that has fins that resemble the ears of the Disney character Dumbo.

21. Glass squid: a deep-sea squid that has a transparent body, allowing it to blend in with its surroundings.
22. Hydrothermal vent: a fissure in the Earth's crust that releases hot, mineral-rich water.
23. Midwater: the open water column between the surface and the seafloor.
24. Mimic octopus: a species of octopus that can change its shape and color to mimic other animals.
25. Vibrancy: the ability of an organism to change color quickly as a form of camouflage or communication.
26. Abyssal plain: the flat, featureless area of the deep sea floor that covers most of the abyssal zone.
27. Benthic: refers to organisms that live on or near the seafloor.
28. Bioluminescent bacteria: microorganisms that produce light.
29. Bioluminescent dinoflagellates: single-celled algae that produce light.

Page |

www.ingramcontent.com/pod-product-compliance
Lightning Source LLC
Chambersburg PA
CBHW012310240726
48656CB00008B/2633